Watched Pots (a Lovesong to Motherhood) Anderson reflects an entire world of mother/child bonding. Memories of the poet's own mother mix in as she heals herself in the midst of needing an extended family while raising a child alone in the heat of the deep south. Much attention is paid to Nature: missing four seasons of change and appreciating her son's attempt to grow pumpkins in the yard comingle with Hurricane Katrina and the child making his first snow angel. Rita is adept at blending the small with the overwhelming and musing that raising a child is as much about lunchboxes and superhero underwear as it is about moving on and letting go with grace. Rich analogies abound—motherhood is *this* but it is also *that*. We are grateful that Rita is willing to create in an unmade bed where passion messes with memories and carries multiverses of Life and Love.

—Donna Hoffman, Artistic Director of W.I.T.

Watched Pots

(A Lovesong to Motherhood)

Rita Anderson

Watched Pots
Copyright © 2016 Rita Anderson

All rights reserved. Red Dashboard LLC
Publisher retains right to reprint book.
Permission to reprint poetry or book must be
obtained from the author.

ISBN-13:978-1-970003-06-2

Photograph © 2016 Steven Robert Anderson
Biography Picture © 2016 Rita Anderson
Taken during Rita's production of *The Second Mouse*, in Paris, France (June 2016)

Published by
Red Dashboard LLC Publishing
Princeton NJ 08540
www.reddashboard.com

For my son—

Seamus Vaughn Anderson

"I'll love you forever.
I'll like you for always.
as long as I'm living,
my baby you'll be."
          Mom
          12/10/16

Acknowledgements

"Alpha Centauri." *Dis-or-der*. Anthology. Red Dashboard Publishing. 2016. Print.

"Caravaggio Paints the Football Stadium. . ." and "Two Moons of August." Poems from my chapbook, *The Entropy of Rocketman*. Finishing Line Press. 2016. Print.

"On Torpor, August, and *Twilight*. . ." *Transcendence*. Spring 2014. http://issuu.com/transcendencemag/docs/transcendence_magazine_issue_1__2_

"Harbinger." *Spoon River Poetry Review*, Volume XXI Number 2. Fall 1996. Print.

"Necessary Procedures." *EVENT Magazine*. (British Columbia) August 2015. Print.

"Object Permanence." *Words Work*. http://wordsworkliteracyjournal.weebly.com/ Volume 5, Issue I. Summer 2012.

"Watched Pots." *Explorations*, University of Alaska Press. 1994. Print.

TABLE OF CONTENTS

Vertigo (1995)

Rises (first[born] baby poem) 4

Harbinger (2001)

Alpha Centauri 20
Aubade 21
On Torpor, August, and *Twilight* 22
Cabin Fever 23
Disappearing, the Sea 24
Harbinger 28
On Helen Keller's, Water! 29
Narrow Escapes 31
New Fences 32
Object Permanence 34
On the Eve of an Almost-Disaster 35
Necessary Procedures 37
Watched Pots 38
What We Call History 39

Last Chance Gas (2004)

*Space*Remains* 42
Taps 44

Caravaggio Paints
  the Football Stadium
    A Skyscraper, a Storm 46

A Long Way, Home (2006)

Angela Got Her Horse 50
Feral Wolverine 52
First Resort 54
Happy Horse Garbage 56
Making the Bed 58
Red Light 59
The Empty Pot 61
With All Thy Getting 63

  Others

How many times have I told
    my son… (1998) 68
Snow Angel (1999) 69
Sarah and Isaac (1999) 70
Malachite Beach (2001) 73
The Men at the Pool (2003) 75
Two Moons of August (2014) 77
Hurricane Rain (2015) 79
Protective Coating (2016) 82
To the Tree that Isn't
    Going to Make It (2016) 84
On Returning to a Favorite
    Retreat (2016) 87

from
Vertigo

Rises (first[born] baby poem)

Sown.
The oddest place to be cut
        —you are born—
and sewn.

*

You were born and you shrieked
You shrieked and were born
You are Subject and Object
              (I become me and mine)
                (mine becomes me)
You are flux, your bones
        liquid s t r e t c h i n g

You have a soft spot in your skull
                      (mine's gone inside)
You eat onetwothreefourfivesixseveneight
        nineten(and sometimes
    eleventwelve)times a day
You *are* and yet you change, your bones
        liquid s t r e t c h i n g

You have a cleft in your chin
You eclipse past
You are the present, gone
The future, your presence
"Presenting (so and so)! . . ."

You are bald and have no eyebrows
You are a fireball broke down
        from the cosmos, your bones

               liquid s t r e t c h i n g
Too soon, the alphabet
U, R, Y, I have arms

*

You hated lying on your stomach;
now you spend the day there,
rooting about like a stegosaurus.
Raised. You are up where
you have pushed yourself. Torso arched,
the top of your head bobs over the grasslike
cover of bumper pads. Hovering yellow-green cows
stir when you bicycle them with your feet.
Your long neck swings through the underbrush;
saliva spools down the sides of your mouth. Crane-
like, your head lifts, drops. Jaw open.
Skin rippling over your tiny vertebrae,
you shake   shake   the blue rabbit
stuffed in your jowls.

                car jack
      I think   Loch Ness
               Sphinx
                     Liberty Statue (the opposite
                 of how she was in *Planet of the*
                 Apes, you are not sinking)

Munching, you tire,
your head drops
anchor.

*

Asleep, your mouth works the knots
of milk from my breast. Hair has overgrown
your birthmark: the red country on the back
of your head, your father's coat of arms.
I am a reference point on a map—
You Are Here. We are
a blind groping of the blood, all
we've got. In the sting of your cry
is the promise of your voice.

*

Small fist opens closes
on my lips as I mouth
words; you play
Helen Keller to my Anne Sullivan.
I am part-God. Feel my teeth.

*

Torture adorns the walls. Plaques of errant
medical history stagger about the waiting
room like Stations of The Cross.

A last minute appointment. The oldest
woman I have ever seen waits, ahead
of us, a native New Orleanian. She leans,
speaking French to you, "Vous êtes
très jolie." Ignorant,
your dad and I just smile.
      "Sorry to say it, dear,
      but she looks like him."
--He.
      "She's got your spirit in her eyes though."

--His. He has.
    "I wish people like you, like *us*,
    were having more children than the ones
    who are. I went to Haiti once. Filthy.
    A little boy came with a handful of sand
    and said, 'You likey
    buy Haiti soil?' Sand is free,
    you understand. Goodbye. Bye——.
    Oh, she doesn't know goodbye yet."

*

Chocolate cake presents cards
Your baptism! The public and infinitely
private (*sacred*) celebration of life and
dedication to God—the he*she*it*we*they*
force of love—Who brought you,
my greatest gift, into the world,
lifechanging event of full-star magnitude.
I promise to teach him love.
Oh, Bless the Day! This journey.

*

Breast pump: Rhythmless repetition.
Lean into an adjustable suction.
A sawing action hums. Passionless
progress. Fresh breast juice.
Sparks from a hole in the ground.

*

Someone told me today,

Babies are born to move away.

*

Four months. Feeding you is like putting on
mascara; to do either, I must open my mouth.
Feeding you is guerilla warfare:
we must stay one step ahead.
Solid food—fruits and vegetables,
lightest to darkest. I feed you with my writing
hand. Is squash oranger than carrots?

*

Four and a half months. You sleep
through the night. I cannot.

*

in mirrors
—an indwelling voice—
lives are backwards

*

(back words)
the falling.
In love with
an appearance. Just making
I ought to.
I,
feel that strongly again.

Afraid I will never
Feel the falling.
Start here.

*

If boy plus girl equals happiness
then go to stanza two.

If love comes then goes,
go to the second stanza.

If kissing does not bring marriage
but a baby carriage
then STOP.

*

Mommy's gone and been and done.
Daddy's still sleeping. A big toad
lives in the cave of our buckled sidewalk.
The landlord put the house up for sale.
The mailbox leans. Rustily, I ride my bike.

The streets are awake with overhauling
as owners dole out first aid and last rites.
A thousand yards of gauze spread on
the neighborhood. Pedal away from same,
a flatness: four walls, three figures.
The way I talk is not good enough for company.
I need a very foreign language. *Poetry.*
What I want is change. --How
many miles have we clocked down
these streets, son? Our walks: you out front

in the stroller, from behind I push.
When you were in me, we walked in unison.

I shouldn't be barefaced in the sun.
I don't need to speed the changes.
I know by accident. I have
never been comfortable in my body.

Older women cut their hair. All the time,
getting their hair trimmed, dyed.
I've cut mine. An indwelling voice.
My wallet, empty for weeks.
We have frozen food. Cans and rice.
Welfare cheese with the melting point
of steel.

Exhilarating, remembering downhill
speed, zooming on my bike.
What I have is rented. The gardener
reclaimed the shape of our yard;
for once the place looks nice.
The house is sold.

*

I sang from A to Z, and talked
nonsensically. Read Dr. Seuss
until he had said his say.
(The king of the house you get your way.)
You swung in your swing,
then laid on your back.
We went for a walk.
--I've simply lost track.
You drank all your juice
and played with your food. I let you

smear me for fun, although
it was not my mood. I can't
pick up a book without rhyming sound,
pound for pound. I used to have books,
the crux unrhymed not SING-SONG,
BRING-SONG-STRING-ME-OUT-TO-DRY-
SONG-DRY-SONG.
All alone.
Nobody to phone.
You wanted more; your FILL line
was half-way. I needed a break.
"For Pete's sake!"
My prospects grey.
Desperate, you cried.
Nothing left to do,
I broke down and cried with you.
You discovered boredom today.

*

About you, this gets
less and less.

*

Your father and I lay like two old pennies,
tail to tail. Once upon a time, the coin
flipped head to head: I had a love life.
The soul's imperceptible flux,
a perpetual floating bladder.
I put on my red nightie, clumsy.
He turns to the wall before
going to sleep on the couch:
"To find love like that,

I'm not that lucky."
"Are your parents?"
"No."
I throw the gown in the garbage
with our words.

*

Climbing the planets of your parents,
you are sun-center, our shadow: the moon.
You are the season of our love come home.
Hands on the side of my neck,
you pull me to you, softly blowing bubbles.
Open-mouthed, you bump
my cheek. Your first kiss.

*

On threes, you are lopsided, semi-
sitting, one arm free to bat things.
A tooth (Is it crooked?) cuts through,
seven months on the dot. Curious,
you only want what mommy does
not want you to have. Baby, sweetheart.
Sucking on a washcloth is brushing
your teeth. Half-crawling. Hair for Christmas,
and your two bottom teeth. Venomless serpent,
you ensconce your victim:
a Christmas dome caging a tiny world.
As you try to unhinge your jaw,
saliva sprays against the glass
like the snowstorm you've started within.

*

early born behind ahead now on
the growth chart out of control
sentence You are racing past
punctuation waiting comma period

*

Mirrors fascinate and then shadows.
A complex connection: that flailing
black on the wall is the same baby
who smiles back at you in the mirror,
next to your mama. Discovering light switches
ON—bright
      blink, blink,
smile. OFF—dark,
eyes wide, mouth opens,
giggle. Good morning. We take the extra
mattress from your crib.

*

The pump went back yesterday.
Milk glands, unpicked grapes under my skin.

*

Eight months. A mouthful of teeth-kernels.
Crawling, you will what you haven't
tasted. What's taboo. You ignore the gifts
of expensive toys for the rusty chair leg
where dad sits, talking to you, trying

to write, his back turned. Garbage
basket at his feet. The electrical outlet.
You are a slug coming at the world
tongue first. I never had anything perfect
before.

*

there now. Your body, exhausted from crying.
You suck my milkless breasts as I rock you away
from pain. You are stranded in a place
I can't get to. The first of many. My son,
and my man finally asleep
in opposite ends of the house. I'm
in the middle, catching my breath, my eye-
lashes so tired they hurt. I'm on a treadmill,
it loops and loops. Here,
the humidity curls things: book jackets, yellow
letters from lovers I have stuck on the wall
like a finger rammed into a dike of memory.
It straightens others: hair. In my eyes.
Twigs fall on the mailbox; I think
it's you, waking. *There,*

*

Flash at the moments. Flash.
Flip through blocks of photos,
thumbing the edge—static
figures move like cartoon sketches:
It takes a million to catch one action.

*

Refrigerated chewables.
Orajel. Tylenol.
Enchanting, the teething process.
A Non-Stop Scream Fest.
"Look, Seamus, a bird! Hear
the truck pass by? The neighbors
making love?" It doesn't matter;
like a dog, you only get the inflection.
Patience bankrupt: we are ready
to send you back. You've ripped
off our headsets of ideas. We hear
only the pitch of your pain.

*

Steam hisses from the vaporizer.
Your appetite and fontanel have sunk.
Nine months. Sick, you are the ocean
of a woman in labor; in tortured
half-sleep you writhe, kicking
off the raft of my chest where
I have battened you down to monitor
the tempest of your breathing.
You collapse against me
before jerking again. Morning:
the mirage we're headed for.

*

Today, I gave away what you've outgrown.
Holding each t-shirt,
sock
to my nose (one last time),
I inhale the past

before folding it and bagging it.
"Hang on to your maternity clothes,"
my mother warned. "Or you will
get pregnant again."

*

A tadpole loses its tail.
The physical tie between us
has shriveled off. Somehow,
I don't know when, we changed
places: an invisible string
is in my navel now. Your cry
is the fishing pole that reels me in.
An indwelling voice. My magical
breasts are gone. I'm in my old jeans
again, just a woman, as your
father has always been just a man.
My uterus waits, a secret
I have tucked away.

from
Harbinger

Alpha Centauri

> *Sometimes I think of your body*
> *when I'm on the elevator and I don't*
> *care who sees,* he whispers.

I used to like the idea of our closest star
being eight years away. It made me feel
safe from invasion, or like the news could
finally put a lid on the planet's expansion craze.
In school, the distance was explained as such:
> If we took a picture of you today, *they*
> wouldn't see it until you were eight years
> older and had kids of your own. . .

But I am not into kinky romanticism.
I do not dream of my misunderstood mother
singing an odd love song under the blood moon
in a nightdress, which seems to be the *thing*
these days with the cappuccino set: To date
I've seen five movies and read four books
about people remembering, kindly, their mothers
as midnight snow dancers. I don't find depression
interesting
because my mother was lonely.

When my son was weeks old and blue
from screaming himself into hiccups, I strapped
him into the car seat and drove around barefoot
in pajamas until I almost ran out of gas.

> --Sometimes I want an audience,
> but mostly I don't want witnesses
> and I don't want words
> to make pain beautiful.

Aubade

Courtship was jasmine,
   a garland for dancing, love's
      fire like juice that bouqueted

      from our hands, there
   where roses scalded the fence.
And there, where color and fever threatened

to swallow us, God promised seed
   if we were prepared, to learn: *Pleasure*.
      From the inside. Then, racing

      ahead, from the window we watch out,
   boots scrape down the street as our children run
for the bus. Later still—bodies growing, moving

away—the family gone but in frames and
   days become hours with longer arms
      and legs as wishing

      for a phone call, a promotion, the week-
   end we disappear the years.
: *One must preserve against sunset.*

On Torpor, August, and *Twilight*...

Would you like to swing on a star? I sing,
my son's fever rising; again, I bathe him

in tepid water, pleasuring in the fact that
I am the only one he'll let wash his hair

like a lover's small privilege. *Carry moonbeams
home in a jar?* I would like to send word

from the cool patio of happiness but, usually,
I'm writing towards the mint julep—as if everything

were August, the wicked month, a constant striving
to feel better. *Or would you rather be a fish?*

Ignoring my son who kicks against his crib,
I read the last book Nietzsche wrote before

leaving us for the moon orbiting his mind.
Perhaps now isn't the time: I am not strong

and he's making a lot of sense... But,
when fevered, there's no harm in looking.

(Friedrich, were you severed from family and
so friendless that your senses also left you?)

It's their way, the helpline voice says
when I call. *Children burn up.*

Cabin Fever

*Let's sleep on the couch
like birds in a nest*, my son
snakes in my hands, postponing
bedtime. Although I've flushed
four mammoth roaches today,
I keep the windows open, the air
teeming with the stench of burnt
butter from the coffee plantations
across the lake. *I used to love summer*
but now I harbor a growing
hatred of the South, the oppression
of lushness as one overgrown season
feeds into the next. Six-feet below
sea level, we maintain a half-step's
advantage over nature, our thin
rows of brick, a leaky dam against
the flood of green. I miss a winter
harsh enough to arrest all movement
and most life. My head pounds
from the cacophony of *sameness*,
tired of the outside in my room.

Disappearing, the Sea

> *I didn't know one could lie down*
> *in such swiftly opposing currents.*
>   Robert Hass

In the morning, dressed in yesterday's clothes,
it's, Feelings like a book stolen from a room
that doesn't exist anymore. After coffee
I was thinking, Love is a hill and when you sleep
you note the slant, the soap falling into the sink.

At sunset, the wheeze of air conditioners
easing, I can no longer ward off thoughts
like legs that push off the wall of the present
to strand me near where the condo sits
(a refuge our estrangement has cost me),
the management desperate to regrow
dunes a hurricane bulldozed summers ago
--the season that apathy choked out our hopes--
the dunes little more now than forced slopes
littered with signs threatening legal action,
as frequent as sea oats used to be. The nights
thick with storm, I was unable to bring ours on,
afraid to stay or to finish: I didn't want the purple
horizon any closer and I wasn't ready to get wet.

When I think of that time, I think mainly
of the jellyfish, weaving like water clouds around
our ankles, amazed that I was never stung,
the sand giving way underfoot, where bubbles
          burst painlessly against the toughened skin
from tiny-shelled creatures that surfaced for air
and then burrowed before the next wave.

And, of unquestioned obedience, the hose
on the bottom patio where we were instructed
to rinse our feet before ascending the stairs,
which were coated with sand. How futile the effort
seems now, to keep out nature where we had
trespassed. (There was the usual conflict of desires:
a wish to stay under wraps and a need to swim
blindly.)

Every glance back sends me reeling, the layers
and years unraveling until my mother has fallen
down the basement stairs, her chest soaked with
vomit. *I'll take care of it*, I had assured her, not sure
if she could perceive in her underwater-like state.
Peeling off her soiled gown felt like the times
she had tried to confide in me about her sex
life with my father: I wanted to run from the shame
of her nakedness. --When she woke the next day,
the grey in her eyes like rips in the sky after rain,
I am sure a robin sang out her window like always,
a tired sound, the kind of warble that barely
involves a rising of the chest, but there was no
mention of what we had come to call the Blackouts.

--Faint, I should eat something but I'm not hungry
for what I have in the freezer. With summer
moved in, my appetite has disappeared
as if it were a seagull with a backwards sense
of migration. Not back to Who Am I? but
Where Have I Been? Busy mostly, avoiding
the lies, debris that collects on the bottom
until a storm kicks it up.
                                  You and I fell

into a spin we could not cycle out of.

Losing our foothold, we settled for cozy
deception. You, too, must have felt
the opposite pulls, lit cigarette in hand
on the dark porch, a red glow I used to mark
my departure, the hot tip extinguished
by the time I had passed a first row of houses.

Barefoot in the dark, I struggled, the dry
sand lending me no push. Up ahead,
under the cold caress of safety lights, a boy
shouted, unearthing a partial starfish.
Other children ran to dig up crabs,
dropping them in pails they would abandon
somewhere between the emptied hotels
and packed cars.

      : But recovered memory isn't fact.
      (Are you still in the shipwreck?)
      It isn't recovery.

Not to be lost to the undertow of empty hours,
I save laundry for the weekends. Pulling up the last
load, I watch our son landlocked in the sandbox,
and then swimming in an inflatable pool
with fallen leaves and drowning beetles
as company. I knock over the diving masks
I don't know what to do with and I can't
throw away as if they were unfinished chapters
of a book I can't close.
                        --Our last morning

there, oppression gone from the air,
the green sky giving way to a sunny blue,
an abandoned speed boat had washed ashore,
the early beach already crowded with onlookers.

We moved to the water with a desire to move
together, as if there were a limit to how far
we could let the other drift, the way we had felt
when we first met. That afternoon as I lolled
weightlessly in the salty waves, the warm, lemony
drink of reconciliation coursing through my veins,
I had discovered three masks:
two adult-sized ones and a child's.

At sunset in the bed you later swore we had
conceived in, we wondered what had happened
to those travelers, believing we had found
the only clues to their disappearance.

Harbinger

Dead clover lines the walk like garnish
left on an emptied plate, remnants of our son's
first birthday. Even on the front stoop,

I can hear the workmen out back gathering
chunks from the live oak that shaded our lawn
yesterday. I try not to take everything as a *sign*,

although loss has always been obscene to me
without the cover of metaphor. "I was afraid
it would snap," the landlord shouted, a huge chain-

saw vibrating his arms. You saw only your rage
in his safety goggles. What it took for you
in your robe to rush at him when the noise

woke us before sunrise. The futility of your
embarrassment. How you had to return to the house
empty-handed. When the men drive off, I move

to the woodpile next to the tree stump. Limbs
are stacked like a pyramid, their golden middles
exposed. As I count circles on the wet wood,

I feel you at the dark window behind me.
In your moist fist is the bitter seed of love.

On Helen Keller's, *Water*!

This morning after a fitful night of flu
      my son and I are outside for fresh air,
drawing shapes on the sidewalk. As I
      outline him in chalk, he asks me
where his name came from and I tell him
      while *expecting* I searched for boys'
names but couldn't find one whose origin wasn't
      tainted with memories of a sad uncle
or a kid who was mean in school, wanting
      a *blank slate* that a new soul could
grow into and define.

It's true, but I tell my son this story because I am
      trying to explain how words "work,"
that he can't say, *That is Daddy's word*,
      and *You can't sing that song because
it is Nana's.* I tell him that people don't "own"
      words: We share all kinds of music in order
to communicate. --Then I stop, mid-sentence,
      as if I've fallen through a waterwall of
      delirium myself because I think he's right.

People do *inhabit* *words*songs*smells* all the time--and that without pictures attached to words meaning isn't possible.

Narrow Escapes

> *At least 30 children have drowned*
> *in their diaper pails since 1973.*
> A Parent's Guide to Home Safety

Days she hovers over her son's play
like a referee while he whirls under the arc
of her legs like a croquet ball. Then, he shoots
off, straight for the woodpile!

Now at the window, she shadows him where
right outside a stray cat plays in the grass.
Soon he will be able to ask, Can we leave it
a dish of milk? Peering up at the frenzy
of red leaves that dangle from fingerlike

branches, she recalls Kennedy's *eternal flame*,
waiting for the day--when drifting in her own
thoughts like this one second too long--*her*
vigilance falters and, leaden, she navigates
as the child's screams siren them through
wet streets to the hospital. . .

At night, she reads to him from a cloth book,
the story about ten dogs in a bed with the one
on the end not sleeping, and she is raked
with concern, pressing the question
mark of him to her skin when he wakes.

She lives on guard against dark corners,
sharp edges because as much as you love is
as much as you stand to lose.

New Fences

Before the baby was born, I'd walked hard uphill,
flailing as if drowning, my body an anxious cage.

I watched neighbors pay lazy attention to their
children who fought in the street like leaves

in a storm. (*Would I ever be confident enough
to think that our son could survive without*

constant surveillance?) Years later, I bike
that same street, noting the removal of an ancient

oak in our old yard and how the buckled pavement
that led to our rental had been smoothed. I glide

around the corner to avoid meeting the new tenants,
longing to hear the after-dinner rush of water

down that sink. I circle the block again
and again to wear myself out but the yearning

increases until it is all I can do to keep myself
from barging into *their home* to remove my hair

from our old drain, reclaiming the clothesline
my father had hung for me as a favor. I know

it's absurd but if I could I would distill
from those rooms certain *sounds* we made

while under that roof like the patter of the baby's
first steps on the cracked floorboards. As if memory

was *matter* we could absorb with a vacuum, as if
it were possible to recover this part of lost selves.

Oh, please, *renovate*. Cover the past.
Paint and repaint. Bury it deeper.

Object Permanence

Just as I am sure you must be *around*,
sharing a piece of the invisible universe,
somewhere, a gorilla sweats in the shade,
eating aphids from a leafless stick. . .
Not counting trips to the bathroom,
I am down to four hours of sleep and
when I dream I am with Houdini,
swimming in an ocean of liquid ice.
We keep our eyes open, waving
our hands like windshield blades
to recover the exit in the fist-thick ice
overhead. He is better at floating
close to the top where you can
almost catch a breath between waves,
but it will be over soon: For all of his magic,
there is no escaping an ironic end.
In the middle of the ordeal, I remember that
this isn't my tragedy and I am rescued
to a warm room where I remove my brain
to soak it like you could a pair of dentures.
--In the morning when I slip into the kitchen
to pour my son a second bowl of cereal,
he no longer cries, afraid that because
I have exceeded his sight I've disappeared,
and when my right hand hides the red ball
behind the abyss of my back, he anticipates
the left hand's finding it, perhaps too certain
now of its return.

On the Eve of an Almost-Disaster

my son is choking
        the clock stops   slow motion
heads turn   he reaches for me
        drowning   on dry ground
right in front of me   no air getting in he
        moves his lips unable to cry   terror
in his eyes   paralyzed   by fear I can't
        touch him   damned feet of concrete
            I cannot
touch him   I don't know How? Find a way
        to help him   Help him! I hit him
on the back knowing it's the worst
        thing I can do but I am helpless
not thinking straight not
        thinking   he is red he is blue
he tries to cry I am crying—
        he is buried underground and I can't claw
fast enough as a split second splits into
        a million more as an ordinary "before"
is becoming a tragic "after"   *There is no moment*
        but this and there never will be.
With one finger down his throat   I am
        at the phone dialing   trying to imagine how
I will perform the tracheotomy I saw on TV
        where an off-duty doctor ventilates
some choking guy's throat and puts a straw in there
        and I still don't know what Mimi did but
she sweeps him upside down like a sack of grape-
        fruit and my son is crying   for me he is
crying. He can cry! Because he's breathing
        again. I want to sing! To singe this moment
into my brain and celebrate the anniversary of

the day that God gave my son his breath back,
    giving him back to me.

Necessary Procedures

Because I woke with blood in my mouth
      I am pulling the pins from my hair,
      which falls around my face like a veil.
      I request a lead bodysuit but the X-ray
      technician laughs, wrapping a heavy apron
      around my waist. I want to follow her
      when she leaves the room, but I stay
      in this place of danger for a treatment
      more compassionate than the alternative.
      Abandoned in a sterile room,
      the metal bed and I swathed in paper,
      my body is a piece of science fiction,
      a glowing chunk of meat, a conduit
      for technology. Mouth open, chin
      pressed to the "X," I imagine the smell
      of my son's hair after he has been playing
      in the yard, but when the nurse returns
      for adjustments, telling me she'll have to
      take another shot: *I cut off the top of your*
      head, I join the trees flowering in the yard,
      dusting the world with their fertile saffron.
            Nothing is frightening from there:
not the dials manipulated from behind
a concrete wall or the picture of cancerous
rocks in my head, not even the thought of
touching words scribbled in stone. . .
From a distance, even the rubber gloves
suspended from hooks like severed hands
are pious, five-petaled flowers.

Watched Pots

On Sundays when my son is with his father
I keep busy. There are toilets to scrub, papers

to grade. Ironing. A litany of things in need
of attention, I forward my distraction to them.

But this flurry isn't smokescreen enough
to swallow the loneliness that envelops me.

Finally, I collapse into a chair on the patio
with a drink. The stump of the oak they cut

down last year is camouflaged by a sheet
of flowing green that shot up immediately

afterwards like a scab. I wish I had Nature's
resilience. I wish I knew how to salvage a loss

and spin it off into an altar of healing, but how
can I parlay my mistakes into things of beauty

when I can't even say I've learned a lesson
half the time? The sun has set before my mind

settles, the night breeze blowing through
my blouse. Still, I wait and pray to be tired

enough to sleep. More than another chance
I want wisdom to know what to do with it.

What We Call History

Two sisters with toddlers
the same age hold them,
wriggling, up to the light,
swearing to one another as witness:

> We will *always* remember
> what this feels like
> *--hold my hand and promise--*
> how they were at this age.

from
Last Chance Gas

*Space*Remains*

Up late because of the move, my son
struggles with his homework. Picking

at the edge of his paper, he stares and
erases again. *Finish your water.*

I tiredly unwrap plates, wadding
old newspaper. *My water is forming*

a skin, he peers into the mug, more
interest than disgust. *--Did you know that*

a shuttle was flying through space
when a speck of paint that had gone

galactic hit the windshield? The imperceptible
crack which resulted caused the whole vessel

to explode. Burying my head in the cupboard,
I shelf dry goods, thankful for the light

inside of my son which—although it laid my sins
bare—illuminated every corner of the universe

like the wiry stem in a lightbulb, as if it were
the mechanism of hope itself. *That's intense,*

I manage after considering just how intimately
I understood the dangers of cosmic debris.

Killed by our own junk! Kissing his forehead,
I close his book. *Enough for tonight.*

He points, *Look how still the water is
in this cup. Unlike our lives.*

Taps

In late March, June bugs cling to the screen
even after you tap it. We heard the beetles

before we saw them, quick cracks against the back
glass where blinds obscure the view. I turn off

the porch light to kiss you goodnight, anxious
to return to the music inside, old tracks that remain

favorites, the lyrical meaning changing as I have
with sadness in more places but deeper joy.

Yes, we have *tried it all*, retreating to the woods
to climb steep paths along the canyon which others

have avoided, listening to what the trees had to say.
We built fire and sang songs to solder this circle of

broken spirits we have become. We've even invited
in the silence and entwined ourselves in the season,

hoping that as every earthly thing abounded
we too would be healed, forgetting the dead possum

in the road for the chattering traffic of featherless
birds. *But*. As tough as problems are to resolve,

eradicating a nuisance is easier than the inverse:
Resurrection. --What if the root of the problem is

that there *is* no longer a *root*? The gratitude I feel
when you rid the yard of flying ants does not

translate into attraction. No matter how close
the days, you cannot force spring but merely plant

and wait for the soil's response. Besides, identifying
what intruded is not enough to disable it. Some

trouble grows resistant, exhausting itself to return,
heartier. The only cure to curb the swarming

is to extinguish what drew it here.

Caravaggio Paints the Football Stadium, a Skyscraper, a Storm

In the mind of this dreamer, the only window is closed and seems always to have been so.

I. Stadium

In the backfield, a human tank waits for the snap,
but from here he's all tortured grimace, a dark
smudge for eyes. The turn of last century was

at hand, his family—engulfed by a complex
ensemble—already a thing of the past. Sounds
bounce from miniature speakers over bleachers

of hot dogs and chocolate, but (*to keep an emphasis
on the essential*) the beautiful boy *is* the show. And
here, before love has found him, he allows himself

to slake his thirst and he desires to surpass himself.
The spectators, alive only in their hopes for him,
hold their painted breaths and hang on the edge,

frozen in the stands like a backdrop of rotten fruit
and fake leaves juxtaposed with fresh. . .

II. Skyscraper & Storm

From a top floor of glass walls, the geometry
of downtown and Heaven itself are the backdrop,
au current, to three figures cast in silhouette.

They huddle as a storm erupts from black clouds.
(They too were a city in the throes of
transformation.) "We should get to solid ground,"

he shouts. "Or at least get out of the window,"
she mumbles as father, mother, and son empty
the tower. But each pursues a separate path to

safety. (Was the family tired of a common life and
life in common? Or is theirs the kind of mystical
crisis a painter cannot capture?) Running free now

in the street, they don't see the Lightning Bolt
that comes for them. It splits the sky to end
the chiaroscuro forever, showing us—the

onlookers—that, There's no escaping destiny.

> Foremost in the portrait stands a provocative
> Angel who strokes the Lamb that will
> replace the child.

from
A Long Way, Home

Angela Got Her Horse

Minutes before the alarm the rain
turns to hail and the puppy will not
go outside to *do his business*. Bills
on the island, sixteen voicemail.
--Is the coffee ready yet?

Kissing our son goodbye, I watch
raindrops bounce off of his hood as
he walks down the drive, losing
sight of him before the bus stop,
ours the only porch light on.

In the dark I return to bed, pretending
to have a choice. I've won the lottery!
It's time to retire. Great-Uncle So and So
willed me a carefree life and an antique
shoe horn, the luxury to be mundane,

hours to shop for window dressings,
lunch with the ladies--one new restaurant
a week, a personal trainer, and travel
to Postcard Land where it's green
without rain. Bright beaches, friendly crabs,

not this same grind that silenced my father
and his. (*Tomorrow is Friday*! my son said
at breakfast. *Doesn't that make you happy?*)
I am tired of grammar, and who wants to ram
the significance of *The Crucible* down one

more throat? Last week Ruby told the Sunday
school class her father has cancer. (What if
I just ran away?) And during prayer Angela

thanked God for protecting her family:
*My friends are plagued with hardship
but we have missed the ax yet again.*

I wanted to injure her with Arthur Miller's
point: *Your soul isn't worth testing,*
responsibility making me mean. So you can
take your afternoon naps, your idle collecting,

days spent overeating and dieting, just
hop on your new horse and ride off. Into
The Sunset! --Did you know its colors come
from pollution?

Today, subsistence farming sounds good,
no outside reference or community duty.
Today I'd give *anything* not to have to
slide on shoes, find the keys, cage the dog,
and lock the door behind me.

Feral Wolverine

"I did the math," my son said, taking
the hand I offer to cross the lot that stood

between me and the overpriced espresso
I craved. "You are thirty-eight but that

doesn't make you old." Tired inside
a morning when I felt much older, I smiled

because the sharp mind that sparked tough
questions was producing its own answers.

(*When did that start?*) Had I missed the signs,
moving as he had away from the cartoon

lunchboxes and superhero underwear?
He frowned now at kissing me goodbye

in public, hands in his pockets. "What is the
difference," he blurted, hardbound classic open,

"between Wolverine and Feral Wolverine?"
Feeling like the outfielder who hadn't fielded

a ball in too long and so wanted the big play,
I thought about it too long. "Feral means wild,

returned to his roots." "I know," my son retorted.
"He puts on a mask to hide his face and goes

berserk." Done with the story, my son shelves
the book but, oddly undone, I keep the image of

the wolf-man close, empathizing with the rigors
of maintaining a certain appearance, anxious

to see him revert back to his natural state.

First Resort

Eyes closed, the boy sticks his fingers
    into the box to let them envision
in an awkward act of confidence. Behind,
    his mother held his books, a certificate

that would end up in a ball under the bed,
    a library card, and a pencil he had
earned for reading 400 minutes, her lips
    forming, *Stay here in the moment,*

a mantra that overwhelmed, the eyes
    floating over flat faces that peered
into borrowed computer screens, typing
    nonsense emails if she had her guess.

A line formed to use the computers but
    not a soul walked the aisles searching
for a book to take to the beach to help
    shape the summer hours that slipped away

like the best of intentions. "Did I
    spell this right?" her son asks, pointing
to *spachula* in crooked letters. Then
    he flips his chin towards the woman

who had captivated him, her sleeveless shirt
    and shorts worn to display a formidable
tattoo collection with an air of, *Oh, These*
    old things. All four of her limbs patterned

like wallpaper and proving that anything could
    become background or be taken for granted,
which pulled the mother and her son out of
    that small town and into Melville's novel,

complete with their very own Queequeg.
    "As a first resort, I'd have to say that
that last item is a fork," the boy reasons,
    answers dropped in the guess box.

"We don't say *first resort* only *last*--and
    I don't know why. Let's go," the mother snaps,
taking a final look at the inked woman to eye
    the tattoo unlike the others--the one whose

        meaning the mother understood--a newer,
        handcarved *Joe,* inside a broken heart.

Happy Horse Garbage

File *this*. Sorry but instructions began. Does
anyone have a light? Keep arms and legs in
until the ride comes. In complete sentences!
Down in front: no shirt, no shoes. Stop. Just
drop the "Service" and roll 'em. Please,
tell me if you see problems: err roars.

Remember that we have to have. We also
cannot. If we could. *That* would be excellent.
( ) hasn't returned. My call, mother's milk.
You said you were open. I took advantage.
Accommodate all. Who had responded so?
Dead at 42. Let me know if you see. Problematic

errors. A needle in a record. Broken until death.
Do us. Part. *Is this on the test*? If one is inspired to.
Vary. It's the Law! Paper needs. The Surgeon
General warns. --*A light?* Label both as follows:
Love. For some reason. Honor the dignity of others.
Will not fit inside the box. Outside Cleveland,

sixteen inches. Freeze dried. *Kisses.* The baby's
cloth horse spoiled in storage: yellow is a sad color.
Children grow. Away from. (What drew us
together?) Prunes in the pantry. People, people
who need. People, It's *not* rocket surgery! The
universe (actual size). In photos. Albums. Old prom

music. Live on stage. Girls! Girls, let the sun shine.
Let the sunshine. In case of emergency your seat
can be. Manufactured in a plant that processes.
Peanuts! Get yours. (If we could.) *Mine*. Finders

keepers. Losers barking up the wrong cup of tea.
Jogging suits, a ten-cent tip, the "k" in knife,
knee-highs. Attention: Love me like that.

In addition, too. *Please*. Nonsense, *are* mice
nesting in your treasure? For clarification. For
the last time. "For all the girls I've loved." Before
and after. Forever. (Does *anyone*?) If we could.
We also cannot. Come for lunch. We'll try. Again?
Far but try and hit the goal.

Caution, there is no place: without magnetism
(*Run away*) gravity cannot bind light life (*with me*)
like a box of take me HOT! chocolate home.

Making the Bed

She said, How long have I been sleeping?
And why do I feel so old? Sarah McLachlan

Making the bed was a simple study
in Before and After. Unkempt, the bed
was a symbol for *chaos*, while fixing its
loose ends with a flat hand lent
a sense of *controlling* the uncontrollable
(*What could be easier?*). Downstairs
within the confines of a twenty-inch screen,
dinosaurs again roared for blood in
a cinematic reality (her son could not get
enough of), thanks to the scientist who had
pulled their DNA from amber-encased mosquitos
who had last dined on them, but today, she
needed no reminder that the universe was contained
within infinite microcosms. Even the comforter
spoke of union and decay, grey hairs of her
husband twined into the fabric next to her longer
strands as surely as—if the technology existed—
filaments of their dreams could be extracted
from the pillows, revealing wishes each had
meant to keep private, the divine stamped
into each mortal atom—mere *dust* of the created,
a portal for the creator. Taking the stairs, she
gripped the railing when an inner reeling sent her
back to the made bed where she lies, undoing
her work. Not that the world would stop spinning
but that her awareness of it might.

Red Light

Stranded on a concrete slab waiting for the light,
    I think, There is nothing new under the
    Texas sun in the blinding heat of summer,
    except to me in the flesh.

Calculating relocation, my husband and I had
    studied maps and chosen a floor plan, but
    dreaming a new life did not build it. (As
    much as we are moved by description,

words can't substitute for experience, the oldest lie:
    *I do not have to travel, having read
    the book.*) In the movie of my life
    that highlights the highlights,

I could easily get it right in a fraction of the time
    at a portion of the price, while reality
    is full of waiting, untidy suitcases in
    a motel off the highway packed with

what ties the old to what is to come. Unsure
    at this busy intersection, my son and I
    wait for the right to cross, his body
    pressed to mine. In front, his small feet

shuffle impatiently, my hand like a seatbelt
    over his shoulder. Amid sunlight that's
    as intense as traffic noise, I am touched
    by the strength of his heart which

throbs under my palm as if I had caged a rabbit or a
> bird wanting flight. (I cannot hold him much
> longer.) My son reaches up to hold my hand,
> completing the connection, a circuitry set

in motion, and as I count his heartbeat, I know he
> can feel mine pulsing in my fingertips,
> which he caresses absently, beat for beat
> exchanged. The moment distills for me

the ease with which he lives, solid in mother's
> comfort, (falsely) sure of my direction.
> Reliant, he already strains for freedom—
> a step out into traffic—but when

the light changes, we move in unison like deer
> scurrying from this backdrop of danger.
> Clearing the crosswalk I steer us for
> "home," my thoughts like an irritation

that builds, invisible until it bursts to the surface
> as knowledge: *The heart is the body of*
> *experience, and I cannot be his red light*
> *forever, protecting him. To learn,*

>> *he will have to travel as we all must, alone.*

The Empty Pot

When I'd suggested to my son that we move
the seedlings from the foyer to the corner of our lot,

I thought I was saying *Goodbye* in the usual,
sheepish way but, in late fall, he marched out

to the spot, arms around the pot as if he were
a giant securing a village. *I love plants, but*

I've never been able to keep one alive, I told
him as I hunted a shovel. *In your first try,*

you have two leafy shoots for two pumpkin seeds.
Still, studying the wind and sky, I was sure I was

setting him up for failure, a familiar lesson. After
we had patted the dirt, I hoped as I tucked him in

that the repotted plants--out of sight--would become
another discarded obsession like magic tricks.

The morning I'd tiptoed over cool dew to find one
shriveled stem, I rushed my son off to school

when he asked if he could water the plants, yet
right before Christmas, we walked out to a pumpkin

patch! When he said, *Look how that one seed split
into three vines,* I thought, He saw growth where

I saw death. When he pointed to the harvest bulging
under leaves the size of elephant-ears, I'd thought,

When did my dreams get so small? Circling his
garden, I stood witness to the wonder of the ancient

earth and an eight-year-old's persistence. Then last
night, frost destroyed the matrix of heart-shaped

leaves and I considered the parent who flushed
the floating goldfish, its replacement in the tank

before the child noticed, but I remembered
the emperor who gave a seed to each child

in the kingdom, pledging the throne to the one who
grew the most beautiful flower: the boy who'd

brought an empty pot won because the seeds *had
been baked*. . . My son cried at first, stuffing frozen

pumpkin leaves into a trash bag while I tackled
tendrils woven into the grass, tiny anchors I had

trouble removing, but then, standing at the kitchen
table where we'd transported the smallest green

pumpkin--our last rescue, he brightened over
the lot, his happiness like a second sun.

With All Thy Getting

> *Wisdom is the principal thing*
> *therefore, get wisdom: and with*
> *all thy getting, get understanding.*
> Proverbs 4:7

Another house for sale down the street,
a friend of her son's. As they turn the
corner, he cranes his head out the back

window for last signs of a boy who
is already gone. This was no military
adjustment, rumor had it, but the first

of a bitter split, the tall grass whispering
of abandonment, neglect. Wasn't it
Thoreau who coined "clothes-horse,"

an expression to describe those who
wore clothes without the shirts or dresses
wearing them, shoulders like handlebars

on exercise bikes that no one rode, the torso
a hanger for what did not define it, no
more than flesh and cotton, *user* and *used*?

A nation sold on that transient mindset,
men and women—with a battle cry of advancing
the self—moved into and out of new cars,

houses, and families like clay figures without—
(*Without what?*). An endless consuming, the
churning need for newness that left you hungrier.

You'll never do that, right? The boy's call
puts her back in the body. *It is going to storm*,
she says. *But we're almost home*. Fighting rain,

she runs to the yard, plucking flowers, a handful
of weeds her husband would mow down. Then,
closing out the wind, she finds the word she sought:

"Without *souls*." --The flowers in a cup
sing of wild beauty indoors, choice in
the absolute, and the open end of possibility.

Others

How Many Times Have I told My Son,
Let's Go! (And Now We Are Going)

Packing, how had I not expected everything
        to become sacred during The Countdown?

Not to feel the pang of the Last Couple of Times
        burning down to Take a Good, Last Look?

Years of hurrying to the grocery for milk and
        runs to the post office have not prepared me

for moving out of the house my son was born in,
        these comings and goings of meaningless

motion, so how am I ready for action that is
        charged with "change"?

        And it is the details that pain me most.

Uprooting means *lessening* one's load, discarding
        the inessential, but how can I throw away

the broken dresser with the attached mirror I have
        not dusted—or erase my son's fingerprints,

a perfect shadow cast of a hand he's outgrown?
        Worse yet how to convince my father,

the laborer, to transport the ruined chest [so
        I don't lose the baby I can no longer hold]?

As I step to *move on* with grace, something solid
        in me knows I cannot hold the past
        even if I held onto it.

Snow Angel

Toddling out of bed and out the door
before breakfast.
First snowfall.
His.

Prints in the snow promise
wet pants, blue fingers,
red cheeks, frozen
ears.

Out the window, he molds
the low row of an abandoned igloo,
plastic sled swooshing
past.

"Will you come and play?"
Yes. Later. Laughter
bouncing off of
the bricks.

> *Us* in one image (**Mom**: Milk, splashing
> in the pan, burns on the coils.
> **Son**: Sweaty appetite under knit
> cap.)

Watching him discover, I am
loved but outgrown
like his handprint
on a mirror.

Sarah and Isaac

God has brought me laughter, and
(all) who hear will laugh with me.
                              Genesis 21: 6

As the three of us approach Toledo, we pass what
we have come to call *your* bridge, a forsaken
drawbridge that spans the Maumee which stretched
out before us to the horizon. Although I knew

the river had been boatless for months, the solitude
of its uneven ice floes, jagged and heaved where the
water had frozen and thawed and refrozen, unsettles
me further. Like the rusted structure of the old

railway crossing above, it is a crude reminder of
change, the *indispensable* need that is outlived, a
function lost. While you are in the air, leaving to
visit your birth father, I am on edge, glad for the

motion towards home—as if we are on parallel
journeys. [But we travel separately, you and I, and
we would arrive at distant destinations.] A pair of
smiling travelers passes Dad and me, obscuring my

last view of your bridge. On their car door in a
child's hand, *Merry Christmas, Aunt Kate,*
is scrawled into the salt film that coats vehicles here
in winter. I look up, knowing the white line that

scars the sky is not a sign from you to me but
another plane's vapor trail, going elsewhere.
This is practice, I tell myself, for the ways I cannot
protect you (*only son, fruit of my womb*),

for all of the places you will go without me.
Must go, I corrected. Out of habit, your father and
I resume the travel games of counting water towers,
saying aloud the strange names of roads like

Fangboner and Monclova. Funny how the tables
are turned, I think. *You*, the one who struggled to
play the alphabet game with us and whose legs
raced to keep up, *are the giant now* above even

the clouds, the road we drove reduced to a racetrack
that would fit in your hand. And still up, up, up you
would fly until the rectangles of roofs—entire
neighborhoods—shrank into lines as thin as string.

Your distance turning our world into miniature,
distorting known objects until they disappear.
         Meanwhile, earthen-bound, what seemed
like a quick jaunt to get you to the airport slows

in our race to return home. Because time is standing
still now, I study the fences that outline farms,
down in places but repairs would have to wait until
spring out here where winter hits the hardest,

flowing fields shocked into rows of stems, where
telephone lines seem the only, tenuous connection.
Then, excited as we exit the turnpike, I can't help
but mumble the Old Testament wisdom of,

The Lord giveth and the Lord taketh away.
As the sun sets on your first night away, even the
blacktop factory at the city limits is made beautiful,
lit up like a village in the distance, its rises and falls

softened elsewhere by darkness. My fears (*Don't
ask me that*) for your safety (*Take me, instead*)
had subsided like water that boils itself out,
love's run-off. I beam back at the day's last light—

a single streak that splits the sky as if guiding your
flight, and I imagine the poetics of the world as you
see it, simply: I spy a black horse by a red barn in
the white field, and The dirty sheep eat the gold

grass that pokes out of the snow in spots. I let
your vision, pure and hopeful, shame me into re-
vision, as I am too often like those fields I stare at
for comfort, numb from the commonplace beauty

that surrounds me. --You are such a part of my
days, son, your questions the map of my musings:
Mom, how can God be jealous? I had not realized--
as I watched what I said and did around you, ideas

like roots I was planting, as closely as I monitored
the food you ate--that you had become my well-
spring too, a source of inspiration like water I
survived on, your voice as natural and as constant

as the heartbeat, forgotten until missed.

Malachite Beach
   (Texas in March)

With eight of us in a van before sunrise,
every inch of space stuffed with gear
and the sleep still in our eyes, we head
for the beach, a day trip, the busman's
holiday. *Who's ready to get out of here?*

When daylight trades black for grey,
you and I console each other: *The sun will
burn this off.* We drink coffee as the children
tell jokes to pass the hours en route, escaping
the city, routine and, finally, the car.

We join travelers who clutter the coast, each
trying to secure a private stretch of nature
even on a foul day when only determination
kept us afloat. Although the weather had not
cooperated, you had thought of (and brought)

everything from kites to foil, a pan and butter
to roast "a bed of cochinas" we never found,
our children harvesting games from their
imagination like fresh fruit from trees
we did not plant. We smiled at one another,
biting our tongues as the older boys struggled
to set up the tarp, and we spread the blanket for
sandwiches and hosted a windy picnic.

Hoping for an eyeful of spring-breakers
busting out of new bikinis, your oldest caved in
and carved himself a girl from sand. More restless
than the boys, you and I gave ourselves a mission,
as if to salvage the adventure. –And, I know

"tradition" is a root, a link, but how long can one
look for a sand dollar, perfect and whole?

But we did, up and down the hard sand of the beach
front, the sea spitting cold. At sunset, we compared
collections--spiral shells, bits of driftwood,
butterflies, and the puzzle pieces of shattered sand
dollars. You were right, *All we found was dead
or broken*, but in our hands I saw our lives,
the beautiful remnants of imperfect selves.

Unable to see the divine perfection in our busy-
ness, we come to find it reflected here, an
unobstructed view, a world where seagull cries
carried for miles against the tireless surf, the colors
of the Man-o-War and the Monarch pervading
through death, each fragmented thread a feather,
a puff of air beneath the surface like the five
minutes of sun we enjoyed. The Creator
reminding us that our lives were mirrors,

as the sun burst through the clouds.

The Men at the Pool
(*Hope, Arkansas*)

Free in his trunks and flip flops, my son
clears the corner to the pool first: *Jump
in! Don't wait for me*, I cheer, the reverse
of my normal rule but, feeling "observed" and
awkward in my swimsuit, I want to slip
into the pool undetected like a sniper
who takes position only after the decoy's
distraction—and my son accomplishes that,
cannonballing into the pool. [So, why
did I still feel so large a target, the bikini
hugging where the hotel towel failed to
wrap me well enough?] Already *seen*, I had
no choice now but to advance sideways towards
an open chair like a crab scooting to safety.

We had waited until sunset to swim but night
offered no *cover*, pool halogens soaking bodies
in light, each new detail of interest to the "regulars"
[Did these guys *live* here?] who stood on sagging
balconies drinking beer in faded trunks they never
swam in. They chainsmoked while I stared back,
on alert for a chance to get wet without notice.

> Hours ago on the road, swimming had
> seemed the ideal way to relax after a cross-
> country drive, a means of exorcising my
> husband's, Be Careful, which hung over my
> head like a *premonition* [but who could have
> factored in these Neanderthals?].

My son and I swim until the crowd thins
when I break Pool Rule #2 and race him
up the wet cement back to our hotel room, a voice,
Wait up!, behind us. I can barely bolt the door
before the voice pounds on it until he tires.

When my son asks, *Do you know these guys, Mom?*
I do not know how to explain the world to him.

Two Moons of August

> *On August 27, 2007, Mars will come within 34.65M miles of Earth, looking like a second moon.*

Joining the porch shadows, I try not to wake
the house I leave behind but moonlight makes
hiding unlikely, its glow too insistent a *theme*
to mention (but I still feel giddy soaking in it).

Never before or *again in this lifetime,* the news
warned, although I had warmed to the idea of
another planet's proximity, always open to
illusion. Waiting and watching, I wrap my

robe tighter despite heat nightfall didn't resolve,
fresh from the dewiness of bed where you dozed,
our dark dance as if in tribute to how the bodies
in space would revolve to find one another

sometime after midnight (a false coupling to fool
the *untooled* eye). Peering now up at our young
dreamer's window, I wondered if I should wake
him for what he wanted to witness, if not celebrate

with his own late-night appearance *(What about
school in the morning?* less complicated than was
rousing him from sleep). Although I was the sole
witness, mine was not a drive *to know,*

the facts as wasted on me as was such lunar
radiance. --I *did* marvel at the sky but always
wound up counting clouds or trying to locate the
only other intruder on the scene, something forlorn

but likewise earthbound chirping from the treetops.
The flight my thoughts took was *anything but*
celestial, traveling instead, too far back... When
reveling in peaceful surrounds I do not get lost

in math or astronomy but in human nature's web.
From the very beginning. It's the puzzle
I return to, a riddle I can't answer:

> Was there any way that first pair could have
> remained in the magnificent garden,
>
> content with their lot? Or, was one bound
> to nurture an ancient need for *more*?

Hurricane Rain, the Final Wave

on Katrina's 10th Anniversary

When the rain started that time, I relaxed,
    welcoming the break it would mean
        in the heat--too many torpid days

    in a row, another month of torturous
temps you could do nothing with in a summer
that collected volume in the corner like cast off

washrags. That night, I watched at the window as a
    parade of drops wiped dust from the street
        where, an hour before, we had strolled

    until you were tired enough to sleep,
teething and feverish in the writhing dance that
infants do on their way to becoming toddlers.

Normally, when rain happened like this—after
    streetlights spark up and the list of Things to Do
        was done—the rain was an intimate.

    It filled a world where I was alone, its
motion standing in my stead, a calm pulse that
let the stillness be *enough*. But then, the rain

wouldn't stop. . . When the rain increased, storming
    through that sleepless night, relief became
        irritation. *Enough was enough.* Living as we

    did in a city that sat below sea-level, every
occupant knew we lived on "borrowed" time,
the best pumping stations in the world unable to

keep up with the influx of water that poured in and
    kept pouring in—until there was nowhere left to
        displace it. Sheets of water pooled until they

        covered the street, and the sweet music of a
    falling torrent pitched to a shriek against
windows, the roof, and the brain like an intruder

hellbent on getting *inside*. When the power went
    out, I hoped it was because the check hadn't
        cleared, but I held the phone anyways

        until its silence unnerved me. —How you
slept through it, safe in an infant cocoon of
dreams, I can't imagine, and I fought an impulse

to wake you, to grip you to my breast, but I was
    afraid my fear would be contagious, a terror that
        wouldn't rest. When what would become

        Katrina rose above the tires on the car,
    lawns flooded together into an unnatural lake
as if Nature was reclaiming this space, I drove up

our grass to park sideways against the house,
    knowing the highest ground I could find
        wasn't going to be good enough. Then,

        before sunrise, when a natural disaster was
    declared and your grandfather came for us
[somehow wending through a back route, despite

a mandate to, *Stay off the roads*], I was sure that,
    This was the end, and in the darkest moments—
        where neither prayer nor tears could find

       me--there was only the joy of you, and
a wave of sadness that I would never see you
walk or hear your voice pick up the narrative of

your own life story.

Protective Coating

This morning as I paint walls,
the sun fills the yard where the world
has come back to life through the power
of rain. Butterflies crowd the lantana
and lizards change hues to hide from
the dogs in a dangerous balance
called *survival*.

This morning, while my husband replaces
the door—sealing broken places with foam—
I make scuff marks disappear. With one brush
stroke, paint covers whispers of shoes
that the new family we once were had
carelessly kicked off there in our rush
to move into the future.

This morning as baby birds noise-out
from fresh nests, I text our son at college.
When he asks me what I'm doing I—inspired by
the Van Gaugh knock-off in the hall, "Starry
Night," which is said to have a smeary sky
because the artist painted through tears—
tell our son the truth:
I am erasing your childhood.

Unlike Van Gaugh, the painting
I do lacks artistry: I am doing it to get
the house sold so gone away are
the sword marks that nicked the halls
as our son flew downstairs with the toy
in his belt, chaotic shadows of long ago
birthday sleepovers where he and his
friends stayed up all night, oily imprints

of hands along the plaster because
our son liked the textured feel.

No, you're not! our son texts back. *You're
sealing them under a protective coating
so that they'll last forever.
That makes me feel better*, I say.
Me too, he signs off.

To the Tree that Isn't
Going to Make It

Standing on the back porch--flagstones
laid during a family project
too many springs ago, I squint

in the sunlight and shiver with cold
but, because I need a break from packing,
I steel my edge with coffee to take

a last look at the yard, which
already feels like it belongs
to someone else. [*Must every poem*

be about me?] Although the drought-
hardy grass had not yet gone
dormant, most of the leaves have fallen,

tiny yellow ovals of last season scattered
like so many lost coins. I smile, now,
at that one rotten squirrel who teased

the dogs—then, with a twitch of its tail,
it would fly up a tree, disappearing
into the ample canopy of oak, as if

this gravity-defying motion was *nothing*.
Ours isn't a big yard but it was
the largest on the block, a silly

detail that made us proud—although
I cannot say we were close to the neighbors.
And, *we* aren't the *same* family

who planted that row of ligustrums
to shade the back corner, waxy bushes
which didn't inspire confidence when

we bought them, but those knee-high
twigs towered now over the fence, almost
eclipsing the chain store that had cropped up.

--That is, all of the ligustrums but the smallest
one that always struggled. Still, it was the heavy-
handed owner on the other side of the fence

who *did the tree in* when he lopped off half
of it while trimming his own bushes. Truth is,
I have rooted for this runt the whole time.

Maybe it hurts to know the tree's fate
because I have a soft spot for the underdog
or because our son was a premie—and

perhaps when the neighbor *accidentally* struck
that final blow to the tree, it played out
like a new battle in an old war—but, really,

it's because I want every living thing to thrive
or at least to get a fair shot at survival.

And because I knew that this is, *Goodbye*,
for reasons other than we're moving.

On Returning to a Favorite Retreat

Acorns ping against the metal rooftops
and children's quickened footsteps fall
below, laughter and a muffled parade
of questions as morning breaks and
families start the day's agenda.

Smiling, I take it all in in small doses
with my coffee. As if fall or the little bit
we get of it wasn't pleasure enough,
I'm nestled in by the lake in Hill Country—
wedged against the notion that *hills*
and *lakes* are like *fall* in Texas,
mysterious realities that defy expectation.

The trees need a trim, my lover said
last night when I pointed out the moon
that broke through the bramble above,
an almost impassable canopy of scrub branches
that flourished on the hillside.

Then to sleep in this strangely familiar
place, an annual oasis where over the years
our son ran the halls and the work
it was for us to keep his growing spirit
contained out of duty to the neighbors
on the other side of the thin walls.

Perhaps I should be upset that
the "maintenance" and "upkeep" fees
are reflected nowhere on the premises.
It's the same cheap carpet underfoot
and the same plastic blinds
cover the windows except where

someone else's child or pet
broke a row while spying out
the wild cats that roamed
in large numbers, encouraged
because they kept other vermin
in check. The kitchen table is stained
in the same places, char marks
where someone smoked
despite the rules. . .

[But, here alone and against all signs
to the contrary, you try to forget the others
who come before and after you
and that their dreams are filled
with the same yearning that turns
into nostalgia with time.]

--While our son is away at school,
finishing college now, it is almost
a relief that this deck is lined with
the same planks he played on
in the second grade when he was shorter
than the railing which fences in the deck
so that no one falls to their death.

It would be a stretch to say that
the property is well-cared-for
just as it's a stretch to say that
we have a clear view of the lake—
but it is more alluring from a distance
than it is up close, as are most things.
And people.

As the acorns fall faster, hitting
harder, I know any ideas for a walk
around the lake are gone because

it's going to rain. [And *rain* like
the *hills*, *lakes*, and *fall* are rare things
in Texas, but when it decides
to rain here it's a full commitment.]

A giant wasp, rusted wings half
up for balance in the wind
and on alert against my presence,
walks the deck perimeter reminding
me that I'm just a visitor and the wasp
calls these moldy boards *home*.

–But an eagle pulls focus, gliding
overhead on a current before
falling back into its undertow, wings
outstretched in acceptance. For now,
it will go where the wind takes it,
the edge of its feathers outlined
in sunlight.

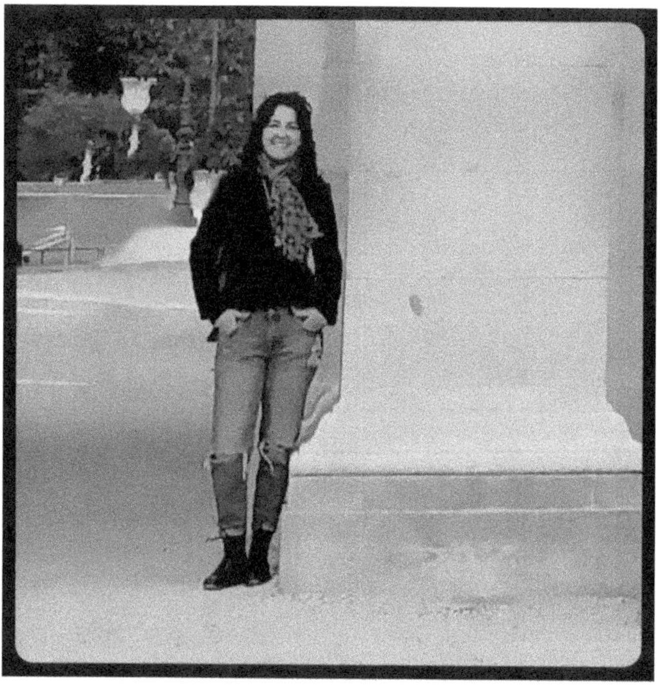

Author's Biography

Rita Anderson, a member of Poets & Writers, Academy of American Poets, and ScriptWorks, has an MFA Creative Writing and an MA Playwriting. A published and award-winning writer, Rita went on scholarship to The O'Neill. Her play, *Frantic is the Carousel*, was the National Partners American Theatre (NAPAT) nominee in 2013, when she also won the Kennedy Center's Ken Ludwig Playwriting Award for "best body of work." She's had numerous productions (to include NYC, Boston, Houston, Dallas, Austin, San Antonio, Detroit, Cincinnati—and in London, England, and Paris, France). *Early Liberty*, internationally published at www.offthewallplays.com, is on their "Best Selling Plays" list. She's on ITN Playwrights Advisory Panel and her plays are available at www.indietheaternow.com but the highlight of her emerging career so far was sitting on a playwriting panel with Christopher Durang.

Rita was Poetry Editor of the literary journal at the University of New Orleans, and her chapbook, *The Entropy of Rocketman*, published with Finishing Line Press (2016). Rita won the Houston Poetry Festival, the Gerreighty Prize, the Robert F. Gibbons Poetry Award, the Cheyney Award, and an award from the Academy of American Poets. Her poems have been published in *Spoon River Poetry Review*, *EVENT Magazine* (British Columbia), *Old Northwest Review*, *Blue Heron Review*, *Ellipsis*, *The Longleaf Pine*, *Cahoodaloodaling*, *The Blueshift Journal*, *Blotterature*, *Words Work*, *Transcendence*, *PHIction*, *Persona* (50th Anniversary Edition), *Di-Verse-City: An Austin Poetry Anthology*, *Inflight Magazine*, *The Stardust Gazette*, and *Explorations* (University of Alaska Press). She was the Featured Poet at FeaturedPoet.com (9/17/16). Contact Rita at www.rita-anderson.com

www.reddashboard.com